IS THE BIBLE FOR REAL?

By DAVID GONZALEZ

Is the Bible for real?

This is an honest question. Many people have asked this question over the last 2,000 years, but it is only recently that people have begun to doubt the accuracy and validity of the Bible. People are intelligent, and they hear many different and conflicting stories concerning the Bible, from social media, movies, books and claims on the internet. You may be one of those people who want to find out more and know the truth for yourself.

The History of the Bible's two sections

When we talk about the Bible, we have to divide it into two sections, the Old Testament and the New Testament. The Old Testament (OT) was of course, written first, beginning about 4,000 years ago. The New Testament (NT) was written beginning around 45 AD through 95 AD. Both the OT and the NT were written as letters to someone, written as a record of past meetings and events, of spiritual leaders, or to a group of people for instruction, correction and direction. The Book of Job in the OT for example, is considered the oldest writing, but not the oldest story in the Bible.

Moses was the first to compile the history of the world into written form. Those books were written approximately around 1400 BC, but were in fact already recorded on tablets of stone or leather animal skins. Moses received a small part of his revelation from Oral tradition[1], and in a large part from direct contact with God. Both God's interaction with him and oral tradition matched perfectly, and as a result, the Books of the Bible that he was responsible for writing (through scribes), are considered not only highly accurate, but inspired by God Himself.

There were two ways for a Book of the OT or NT to be written; the <u>first</u> was from direct contact with Almighty God, as He told the person <u>exactly</u> what to write. In this case, the words written down are not so much inspired, but instead, a direct quotation of what God was saying or directing people to do. The very

---

[1] Written and oral accounts handed down from Noah to Abraham, from Abraham to Jacob and Joseph, and then to Moses.

best example of this is the Ten Commandments. The Ten Commandments were literally written by the finger of God[1], onto the two stone tablets that Moses cut out[2] by God's instructions.

The second method, by which inspired Scripture was written, was by way of inspiration from God, or inspiration from the Holy Spirit. This secondary way that Scripture was written, occurred sometimes as a man having a vision or dream[3], and writing to the best of his human ability, the experience of the dream and its meaning. In this case, we can have interpretation discussions as to the meaning of the Scripture, the Book, or the verses.

The History of the Old Testament (OT)

There are 39 Books comprising the Old Testament, and Moses is known for having written the first five Books of the Bible. Those five books are known as the Pentateuch, "Pentateuch" being a combination of two Greek words, meaning 'five scrolls'. Those books are: Genesis, Exodus, Leviticus, Numbers, and

---

[1] Exodus 31:18

[2] Exodus 34:1-4

[3] Genesis 41:5, 28:10, Matthew 1:20

Deuteronomy. Moses was born in Creation Year (CR[1]) 2368, or about 1500 BC.

King David (of David and Goliath fame) is known for writing about 75 of the 150 Psalms. His son King Solomon wrote 29 of the 31 chapters of Proverbs. Solomon also wrote many Psalms, the Book of Ecclesiastes, and Songs of Solomon. Other well-known authors are Daniel, Jeremiah, Ezekiel, and Isaiah. All these writings, became more or less accepted, over a period of hundreds of years, and examined by tens of thousands of Jews, who were responsible for the accuracy and validity of any writings. Over time, the writings that appeared misleading or inaccurately portrayed God, were unceremoniously eliminated from religious thought and teaching. Prophetic announcements that came to pass were also considered valid additions to scripture. From this time period, no writings survived that were not in ancient Hebrew[2].

---

[1] Creation Year is my system of counting from the Day of Creation forward, using the Bible's birth dates and life spans, to calculate years from the Creation of the universe. We are now at approximately 6,000 CR.

[2] The exception to this is the Septuagint, meaning 70 (writers). This was the Hebrew Bible written into Greek around 200 BC, for Hellenized Jews living inside and outside of Israel. This codex is used today in many Bibles.

The Benefits of a Hebrew based language of the Bible

The accuracy of the OT was very important to the Jews. Non-Messianic Jews only consider the Tanakh, what we as Christians call the Old Testament, as valid Scripture. The Tanakh, which is written in Hebrew, is traditionally written on a scroll. There are 22 letters in the Hebrew alphabet[1] and each Hebrew letter has a numerical value. When a written section of a scroll was completed, a scribe would add all the numerical values of every letter and word, add the columns of numbers, and that section or page would have to match a recognized value for that section. IF IT DID NOT MATCH EXACTLY, then the page would be carefully destroyed, by digging a hole in the ground and burying the page, scroll, or scroll section.

Torah scrolls, as they are called, were made out of kosher animal skins, such as sheep, goat, or cattle. It would take about 80 animal skins to complete an entire Torah/Tanakh Bible scroll.

The other benefit of the original Hebrew is that ancient Hebrew words build upon a parent root (a

---

[1] The English word for alphabet, comes from the first two letters of the Hebrew alphabet, Aleph and Beit.

short root word), and will carry distinct similar meanings. For example, the Hebrew words for <u>sea, water, and heavens</u>, are nearly identical. Water is in the sea, which also makes up our atmosphere.

The benefits of ancient Hebrew appear also in the New Testament, as when a Hebraism appears in the Greek, Latin, and English texts. Because of the style in which Biblical Hebrew is written, and the format of its sentence structure, it becomes clear to Bible scholars, when the original speaker or writer was speaking or writing in Hebrew.

<u>The reason for the Begats</u>

Ever see a movie or read a book, where some young kid is forced to read the 'Begats' in the Bible? Well, the word 'begat' appears 225 times in the King James Bible, and it simply means, in more modern English, "was born to", or "was born of".

It's hard to watch some old preacher in a movie, attempt to sway his congregation with reading such passages, simply because they are not there for preaching, but for the recording and numbering of years and generations, going back to the Garden of Eden. We can count forward from the first week of

Creation to the Flood of Noah, and know, without a doubt, that it was in Creation Year 1656 when the great world-wide Flood occurred. Those that painstakingly study these little clues discover the validity and hyper-accuracy of the Bible.

With all the 'begats', 'begots', and 'begets', we can accurately date the spiritual and historical events of the Bible, and easily match them to non-biblical historical documents. The birth dates and years lived of Biblical characters give us context for each generation. My study of such, has produced notable insights including: Noah was alive when Abraham was born[1], and Noah's son Shem, who was also a witness of the pre-flood world[2], was still alive when Abraham's son Isaac was born. It's fascinating if you think about it, that Abraham sat at the feet of Noah, and heard the "wild-west" stories of the pre-flood era from personal experience; a time gone by!

---

[1] Noah was born in Creation Year (CR) 1056, and lived till CR 2006. Abraham was born in CR 1948, and was 58 years old when Noah died. The Ancient Book of Jasher (9.1-5), states that Abraham lived with Noah and his son Shem for over 10 years. The book of Jasher is a historical document that has survived for 3000 years, and is referenced three times in the Bible.

[2] Shem was born in CR 1558, and was 98 years old at the time of the Flood.

The History of the New Testament

The first Book recorded of the New Testament was the Book of James, written right around 45 AD. Modern calendars concerning the crucifixion of Jesus, used to say that He died on the cross in 33 AD, but that supposes that we started our modern calendars right at His birth, which we did not. Jesus was probably born in 4 BC, and many historical documents such as Josephus, a Jewish theologian and writer born in 30 AD, relate the research of Pilate and Herod's reign to match the 4 BC date exactly. Meaning, Jesus dying at age 33 in 30 AD, gives us a timetable to see how long a NT book was written after His death and Resurrection.

The Book of James was the first to be written in about 45 AD, 15 years after Jesus' death and Resurrection, and the last NT Book written was the Book of Revelation in 95-96 AD. Many of the writers were the original disciples, and I believe that they waited to record the events of Jesus' earthly ministry, until there was a demand for static and reliable documentation of His ministry.

There were other scrolls or books that didn't appear to be inspired, and there were also forgeries; books

Who Approved these Books to go into the Bible?

So, who picked these Books? The New Testament considerations for inspiration and authenticity were;

1. If they were written by eyewitnesses of Jesus' ministry.
2. If the writer was closely associated with one or more of Jesus' original disciples.
3. If the debate over centuries validated or eliminated the books under consideration.
4. If it was found to be with other false and counterfeit writings.

Much debate over centuries validated or eliminated books under consideration.

For example, one early church father, "Irenaeus", St. Irenaeus of Lyons France[1], did that part very well. As an early Bishop of the Christian Church, he wrote essay after essay, and letter after letter, which have been kept uncorrupted. You can buy his now famous book, AGAINST HERESIES[2], and read his written arguments and fearless attacks toward those who would attempt to destroy the Gospel with false and

---

[1] St. Irenaeus, 130-200 A.D., Bishop in Lyons France

[2] 660 pages, available online.

that were written with the express purpose to discredit The Way[1]. That the four Gospels and the other 23 NT books are inspired is reassuring to Christians today. The Gospels cover the ministry of Jesus, His birth, but very little of His early years. And, all four focus almost one-third of their insights into the last several months of His ministry, just before going to the cross.

Q: How could you tell a forgery?

A: Writing style was the best way. Did it match up with OT prophecies concerning the coming Messiah? Were there additions to the scroll or letter added later on? Was it mocking the Deity of Jesus Himself? For over two hundred years, the early church debated about what was authoritative, what was just a historical document, and what was fabricated or uninspired.

---

[1] The use of the phrase "The Way" was common among Believers in the Early Church as found in the Book of Acts 9:2, 19:9, 23, 22:4, 24:14, 22. The etymology may be from the OT Scripture concerning discussion of John the Baptist used in Matthew 3:3, Mark 1:3, and Luke 3:4, from the book of Isaiah 40:3, "Prepare ye the way of the LORD"

counterfeit writings. He was a very serious student of both the Old and New Testament writers.

Other early church fathers were closely associated with the first disciples of Jesus. Clement of Rome[1] personally knew the apostles Peter, Paul and John. Polycarp[2] and Ignatius[3] had working relationships with the apostle John as well. Tertullian[4] and Origen[5] had direct relationships with others that were only one or two generations away from the original disciples. All that interaction with the Eleven Disciples, including Paul and others, played an integral part in determining what was invented and what was true, about the life and ministry of Jesus.

If someone started a church in the later part of the first century, and was teaching something new or strange, all you had to do was to go back to the apostles Peter, Paul, or John, and ask if it was sound doctrine. Later, as those most closely associated with the first disciples, who also became disciples themselves, they also could give the same kind of

---

[1] Clement of Rome, died 99 A.D.

[2] Polycarp, 69-155 A.D.

[3] Ignatius, 35-108 A.D.

[4] Tertullian 150-240 A.D.

[5] Origen 184-253 A.D.

approval or disapproval, of any kind of teaching within the Christian church.

In just a few generations, the Books of the New Testament, as we know them today, survived this lengthy and rigorous testing and approval, before being considered authoritative and authentic.

Why Both Testaments?

Many people, including myself at one time, have asked the question, "If the New Testament tells us everything that we need for Salvation, then why should we read the Old Testament at all?" There are several answers to that question.

First, how can we trust that Jesus was the Expected Messiah without first examining the prophecies concerning Him in the OT? Over one third of the OT concerns future coming events, including the Life and Ministry of Jesus. Jesus fulfilled over 100 Old Testament prophecies, including where He was to be born, where He would live for a time, what He would be called a resident of, and what line of David He would come from. The odds of all that happening with one Man is astronomical, and impossible, were it not of God.

Second, both Books combined give the whole story of Creation, life prior to the Flood, and prophecy concerning the coming Messiah. We can rest assured that we have a glimpse of how well or how poorly ordinary people lived and how they understood and obeyed God, according to the directives from Him and His prophets.

Third, the New Testament ratifies the Old Testament. It confirms the validity of what was said from both directions. I can look at the OT through the eyes of the New Testament, and I can look at the NT through the eyes of the OT, and both validate each other with extraordinary vision and insight.

Fourth, both Books point to coming events through the prophecies recorded in both Books. Ezekiel, Isaiah, Daniel, and Zechariah in particular (though not excluding any others), give a vivid picture of comings events. The prophecies spoken by Jesus in the four Gospels of the End-of-Days, and the Book of Revelation, expound on these same events. Those events are; the Rapture of the church, the Seven Year Tribulation, the Millennium Reign, the White Throne Judgment, and the New Jerusalem[1]. These incredible

---

[1] See my in-depth series called THE SEASON OF HIS APPEARING, 12 DVD or CD set, ©2016

insights give us peace, direction, and a view that God is still in control, no matter how out-of-control the world may seem at times.

This big-picture gives us confidence about our origin, our purpose in life, our Salvation, and Eternity with God. It soothes the intelligent mind with valuable data. It answers the questions, "Why am I here, and, what am I supposed to do with my life?"

The Apocrypha, the third and sometimes excluded section of the Bible

There is a third group of books that only recently have been removed from some editions of our modern Bibles. This grouping of 14 books is called the Apocrypha. The Apocrypha was written during the Old Testament time period and was considered to be inspired. Today, these books are treated as inspired or just historic, depending on your denomination. The Apocrypha was first included in the Hebrew and Greek versions of the Old Testament, and later in 405 AD, were included in the Latin Vulgate translation. The Latin Vulgate had 39 OT books, 27 NT books and 14 Apocrypha books.

Beginning in the late 1300's, German and English editions of the Bible were written and published, with the 14 Apocrypha books in all of them. These complete Bible editions were;

1. The first handwritten English version, the Wycliff Bible in 1382.
2. The first printing press edition of the Latin Vulgate, the Gutenberg Bible in 1455.
3. The first complete printed English version, the Tindale and Coverdale Bible in 1535.
4. The Matthew-Tyndale Bible in 1537.
5. The Great Bible, the Anglican pre-King James version, authorized by King Henry VIII in 1539.
6. The first Protestant Reformation version, the Geneva Bible in 1560.
7. The King James Bible in 1611.

The Apocrypha was removed from the King James Bible (KJV) in 1881, called the revised (RV). All modern versions the Bible had the Apocrypha as recently as 140 years ago. The denominations that continue to carry this third group of books are the Anglican Church of England, the Greek and Russian Orthodox churches, the Coptic Church, the Roman Catholic Church, as well as other minor denominations.

The Apocrypha is an interesting read. You may notice that scholarly Bible teachers will sometimes reference these books in a sermon suggesting the wisdom of the quotation. In conclusion, some people consider these books to be inspired, and for others, just good reading.

Is everything in the Bible a type of everlasting and eternal truth?

No. For example, the stories may in fact be true, but the poor conduct of the men and women being illustrated, in no-way validate that type of behavior, or what they said. Many times, you'll hear Christians quoting a scripture, and it may sound like God, but it was something said in haste, or in error, by one of the thousands of characters being written about.

The things written in the Bible are there for us to use in our lives. The Bible is our manual for us to live our lives. God's instructions for life, such as for marriage, integrity and spirituality, are a guide for us to have a richer and more pleasant life. The Psalms in particular, show us how to honor God and give Him praise. Proverbs shows us how to behave, and how to receive and appreciate Wisdom.

Many of the renowned prophets and leaders in the Bible were just men, subject to the same temptations[1] and failures as the rest of us. So, when they spoke in their distress, it was not God speaking but them. Many times, you'll see daily Bible quotes on calendars, or in on-line posts, that make it appear that God was the speaker, when in fact it was a downtrodden man or woman in despair.

Here are some examples:

1. Job 3:1, *"Afterward Job opened his mouth and cursed the day of his birth."*
2. Jeremiah 20:14, *"Cursed be the day when I was born; Let the day not be blessed when my mother bore me!"*
3. Job 2:9, *"Then his wife said to him, "Do you still hold fast your integrity? Curse God and die!"*
4. Isaiah 6:5, *"Then I said, "Woe is me, for I am ruined! Because I am a man of unclean lips, And I live among a people of unclean lips; for my eyes have seen the King, the Lord of hosts."*
5. 1 Kings 13:18, *"He said to him, "I also am a prophet like you, and an angel spoke to me*

---

[1] James 5:17 Referring to Elijah

by the word of the Lord, saying, 'Bring him back with you to your house, that he may eat bread and drink water.'" But he lied to him."

These narratives of what was done, or what was said, were written to give us context and reveal attitudes. The best way to understand accurately what was being said, is to read the verses and chapters before and after the Scripture being used, researched, or quoted.

Is everything in the Bible supposed to be followed as a modern Biblical command or rule?

No. In Leviticus, it says, you are not to trim off the edges of your beard[1]. But, in the same chapter it says that you are not to turn to mediums and spiritualists[2]. The first is impractical, since it was a Mosaic rule, therefore it was only meant to be temporary; but the second is an everlasting command because it deals with witchcraft, which can be found in various places throughout in the Bible.

Many of the OT rules still stand however, such as; Those about stealing[3], lying and cheating your

---
[1] Leviticus 19:27
[2] Leviticus 19:31, Deuteronomy 18:10,14, 2 Kings 21:6
[3] Exodus 20:15

neighbor[1], those concerning adultery[2], moving an ancient landmark, those about murder[3], and those regarding the welfare of widows and orphans[4]; all these still stand and apply to you living a Godly life.

What Bible interpretation is the best one to read?

Good question. The best way to know what the original texts meant, is to study Hebrew and Greek for the next 20 years, then go back and re-read and re-examine the entire Bible. Even then, you will interpret it according to your understanding of God and people, using your Western mindset. This can, as it sometimes does to all interpreters, move the meaning of a verse to the right or to the left. But there is another way...

Have several different Bibles at your disposal to read. I prefer using the following Bibles for study and background reference: the New American Standard-NASB and NASU, the King James Version-KJV, the Amplified-AMP, the Complete Jewish Bible-CJB, and the World English Bible-WEB.

---

[1] Leviticus 19:11

[2] Proverbs 6:32, Deuteronomy 5:18

[3] Deuteronomy 5:17

[4] Exodus 22:22

In addition, I personally study the original Hebrew to uncover the Semitic thinking behind the verse. I also look at the Hebrew words to see how they are used elsewhere in the Bible. I use many reference works such as; Matthew Henry's Six Volume Commentary, Josephus, Eusebius Ecclesiastical History, the Bible Knowledge Commentary, the Henry Morris Study Bible, and the Complete Jewish Bible Commentary. All these sources help to better understand the Bible.

In Conclusion

All this information serves to let us know that Bible scholars and committed men of God have repeatedly validated and verified the integrity of the Old and New Testaments. Since the beginning of Creation, there have been many men who were willing to work hard at protecting the legacy of the Scriptures, striving to preserve God's interaction with His people in the world.

Consider Eternity with Jesus...

Have you ever asked the question, **"Where will I go when I die?"** You can know for sure, where you will go after this present age, and you can have eternal security. The way to know that you are Saved, and that you have been forgiven of your sins, comes from what the Bible has to say on the subject. Jesus said, *"In the same way, I tell you, there is joy in the presence of the angels of God over one sinner who repents."* Jesus also said, *"All that the Father gives Me will come to Me, and the one who comes to Me I will certainly not cast out."*

Jesus wants a relationship with us, *"Come to Me, all who are weary and heavy laden, and I will give you rest. Take My yoke upon you and learn from Me, for I am gentle and humble in heart, and you will find rest for your souls. For My yoke is easy and My burden is light."* Matthew 11:28-30

In John 10:9-11 Jesus said, *"I am the door. If anyone enters by Me, he will be saved, and will go in and out and find pasture. The thief does not come except to steal, and to kill, and to destroy. I have come that they may have life, and that they may have it more abundantly. I am the good shepherd. The good shepherd gives His life for the sheep."*

Today, we are seeing alarming things happening in the news worldwide. I believe we are living in the prophetic end-times and that Jesus is coming back very soon. In both the Old and New Testaments we read of perilous times prior to the returning of Jesus Christ. However, Jesus tells us not to be afraid, ***"You will be hearing of wars and rumors of wars. See that you are not frightened, for those things must take place, but that is not yet the end."*** (Matthew 24:6).

We do not know the day or the hour that Jesus Christ will return for His Church, but we do know from prophecy, if we have received Jesus as our Lord and Savior, then we will be caught up with Him. His end-time wrath is soon coming upon the whole earth, but those that are saved, won't be here on the earth to experience it. Concerning this it was prophesied, ***"Come, my people, enter into your rooms and close your doors behind you; hide for a little while until indignation runs its course."*** Isaiah 26:20.

You can know that you are saved when you accept Jesus as your personal Lord and Savior. Why not make a confession for accepting Jesus right now? Repeat this out loud,

<u>*"Dear Jesus, come into my heart right now, and make me a new person, a new creation. I do not want to be that old person anymore. Thank you, Jesus, for dying on the cross for me, so that I don't*</u>

__have to die, for all the things that I have done wrong, in Jesus' name, Amen. Amen"__

Congratulation! If you just made that personal confession for Jesus Christ, contact us right away, and we'll send materials your way to help you grow in your new way of life. We will also help you find a good church to plug into, so that you can grow in your walk with the Lord.

Is The Bible For Real?

Copyright © 2022 by David J. Gonzalez
ISBN 978-0-9741561-6-3

All rights reserved. No part of this publication may be reproduced, stored in a retrieval system, or transmitted in any form or by any means - for example, electronic, photocopy, recording - without the prior written permission of the author. The only exception is brief quotations in printed reviews.

Additional Resources by David J. Gonzalez

"There Are No Space Aliens" book
"30 Days Praying The Our Father" book
"Who Were The Nephilim" book
"All About The Holy Spirit" DVD series
"These Last Days" DVD series
"The Power of The Prophetic" DVD series
"YHVH - The Hebrew Name of God" DVD series
"CREATION - I Know Who Made That" DVD series
"HEALING!" DVD series

Hundreds More Online
MountainFaithChurch.org

David Gonzalez Ministries
PO Box 847, Lake Delton, WI 53940
Physical Location
11104 Moon Road, Baraboo, WI 53913

www.ingramcontent.com/pod-product-compliance
Lightning Source LLC
Chambersburg PA
CBHW011614290426
44110CB00020BA/2588